Sports Great

PEYTON
MANNING

FOOTBALL

SPORTS GREAT TROY AIKMAN
0-89490-593-7/ Macnow

SPORTS GREAT JEROME BETTIS
0-89490-872-3/ Majewski

SPORTS GREAT DAUNTE CULPEPPER
0-7660-2037-1/ Bernstein

SPORTS GREAT JOHN ELWAY
0-89490-282-2/ Fox

SPORTS GREAT BRETT FAVRE
0-7660-1000-7/ Savage

SPORTS GREAT BO JACKSON
0-89490-281-4/ Knapp

SPORTS GREAT JIM KELLY
0-89490-670-4/ Harrington

SPORTS GREAT PEYTON MANNING
0-7660-2033-9/ Wilner

SPORTS GREAT DONOVAN MCNABB
0-7660-2114-9/ Steenkamer

SPORTS GREAT JOE MONTANA
0-89490-371-3/ Kavanagh

SPORTS GREAT JERRY RICE
0-89490-419-1/ Dickey

**SPORTS GREAT BARRY SANDERS
REVISED EDITION**
0-7660-1067-8/ Knapp

SPORTS GREAT DEION SANDERS
0-7660-1068-6/ Macnow

SPORTS GREAT EMMITT SMITH
0-7660-1002-3/ Grabowski

SPORTS GREAT HERSCHEL WALKER
0-89490-207-5/ Benagh

SPORTS GREAT KURT WARNER
0-7660-2034-7/ Rekela

For other *Sports Great* titles call:
(800) 398-2504

PEYTON MANNING

Barry Wilner

—SPORTS GREAT BOOKS—

Enslow Publishers, Inc.

40 Industrial Road   PO Box 38
Box 398   Aldershot
Berkeley Heights, NJ 07922   Hants GU12 6BP
USA   UK

http://www.enslow.com

Library of Congress Cataloging-in-Publication Data

Wilner, Barry.
    Sports great Peyton Manning / Barry Wilner.
        p. cm. — (Sports great books)
    Includes index.
    Summary: A biography of the Indianapolis Colts quarterback, whose father was also a professional quarterback.
    ISBN 0-7660-2033-9
    1. Manning, Peyton—Juvenile literature. 2. Football players—United States—Biography—Juvenile literature. [1. Manning, Peyton. 2. Football players.] I. Title. II. Series.
GV939.M289 W55 2003
796.332'092—dc21
                                                    2002008394
Printed in the United States of America

10 9 8 7 6 5 4 3 2 1

To Our Readers:
We have done our best to make sure all Internet Addresses in this book were active and appropriate when we went to press. However, the author and the publisher have no control over and assume no liability for the material available on those Internet sites or on other Web sites they may link to. Any comments or suggestions can be sent by e-mail to comments@enslow.com or to the address on the back cover.

Contents

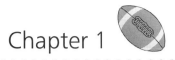

Chapter 1

The Number One Pick

As NFL commissioner Paul Tagliabue approached the microphone at the NFL draft, football fans throughout the nation held their breath. It seemed certain that one of two hotshot quarterbacks would be chosen. One was Peyton Manning of Tennessee. The other was Ryan Leaf of Washington State. Those watching on television at home wondered which would become the first pick in the entire draft. The fans in the stands of the Theater at Madison Square Garden were chanting the names of either Manning or Leaf.

Through the years, there have been many great quarterbacks who did not have the honor of being the No. 1 draft choice. Dan Marino went late in the first round of the 1983 draft. Joe Montana was not selected until the third round of the 1979 draft. Other star quarterbacks such as Brett Favre, Doug Flutie, Mark Brunell, and Kurt Warner were not even taken in the first round, let alone at the top of the entire draft. But either Manning or Leaf would be.

"It would be special," Manning said.

"Anybody would like that," added Leaf.

The Indianapolis Colts, who owned the top pick, were not giving any hints as to which one they would select. "We have all the information we need about their physical condition, and a pretty good idea of their potential," said Colts president Bill Polian, who would make the pick. "Information is still incomplete on both quarterbacks and we're still evaluating them. What we do know is they're both good players and both will play well in the league."

Playing well in the NFL is not quite good enough for the first overall pick. He needs to be a star, a leader, and—eventually—a champion.

John Elway was. So was Troy Aikman. And Terry Bradshaw. Each was the first player taken from their drafts, and all retired with championship rings.

"For us individually, it's too much for us to put that pressure on ourselves, but, obviously, that's the goal: to have a career like Elway or Aikman," Manning said. "I don't feel the pressure to be the next Marino, Elway or Young, but I'd love to have that kind of career. I kind of put that pressure on myself. I want to play as long as those guys did, and I want to be as good every year."

Peyton's father, Archie Manning, was the second overall selection in 1971. Although he was twice a Pro Bowl quarterback and ranked among the top players of his time, his pro teams never had a winning record and he never made the playoffs in the NFL. Archie certainly wanted his son to have a more successful career—beginning with being chosen before everyone else in the draft. He expected it to happen.

"Teams today have a better chance of turning things around than we did in the 70s," Archie said. "There's the draft, free agency. . . . It reminds me of when we were kids and choosing up sides. That's what NFL teams are doing now, and I think it's a big factor in turning it around."

Ryan Leaf (left) and Peyton Manning (right) together at the 1998 NFL Draft.

Both Manning and Leaf were spectacular in their final college seasons. After Manning passed up the chance to turn pro before his senior year, much was expected from him. He produced by leading the Tennessee Volunteers to the Southeastern Conference title and to the Orange Bowl.

Leaf was not nearly as well known before he carried Washington State, normally an outsider in the Pacific-10, to the conference crown and a spot in the Rose Bowl—the Cougars' first in fifty-seven years.

Once Leaf announced he would skip his senior season and turn pro, everyone rated him or Manning as the top prospect. That they played the most important offensive position in football made it certain they would go 1–2 in the draft.

But which way?

Both players put on quite a show at their personal workouts. Leaf displayed a stronger arm, but Manning had a better touch on his throws.

In the final days before the draft, fans viewed the decision of Manning vs. Leaf as if the quarterbacks had some sort of feud going on. The players knew otherwise.

"His dream was to play professional football, and so is mine," Manning said. "We're not competing with each other until we have to play each other."

Still, only one of them could be the No. 1 pick. Both understood that as Tagliabue made his announcement.

"With the first pick in the 1998 NFL draft, the Indianapolis Colts select Peyton Manning, quarterback, University of Tennessee."

Manning did not jump for joy or yell. He smiled and walked to the middle of the stage. There, he shook hands with Tagliabue and held up a No. 18 Colts jersey.

"Today is just the beginning. This is when it all starts," Manning said.

Peyton Manning holds up an Indianapolis Colts jersey with his name on it shortly after the Colts made him the first overall pick of the 1998 NFL Draft.

"It was close, but Peyton has been a consistent leader for years, has produced under a lot of pressure and has showed maturity beyond his years," Colts owner Jimmy Irsay said. "The fact he went back to Tennessee for another year tells you he's got great integrity. And he's had the chance to learn the game from a young age. He's known longer than most players what he wanted to do."

Chapter 2

Family Life

The Manning family always has been close, and a strong part of the bonding has been football.

Archie Manning was the greatest quarterback—and probably the best overall player—that the University of Mississippi ever had. Olivia Manning was the homecoming queen at Ole Miss, married the star football player, and then set about raising a family to be proud of. Archie and Olivia Manning would have three sons: Cooper, born in 1974; Peyton, born in 1976; and Eli, who was born in 1981. All three boys virtually grew up with a football in their hands.

After college, Archie Manning starred for the New Orleans Saints in the NFL. He also later played for the Minnesota Vikings, although he never got into the play-offs. Some people consider him the finest pro quarterback never to make the postseason.

While Archie and Olivia were encouraging their children to enjoy sports, they also were instilling in them the proper values. It is something every coach who ever worked with Peyton Manning will mention. It is something Archie and Olivia take great pride in.

Archie Manning is shown here in action for the New Orleans Saints in November 1973.

"Football was never the most important thing in raising our children," Olivia Manning recalled. "If Peyton had never played football, that would have been fine with us. We only wanted them to do what they wanted to do."

All of the boys played a variety of sports. Peyton participated in baseball and basketball, but always found football the most enjoyable.

Except, that is, for the one year the family spent in Minnesota after Archie had left the Saints for the Vikings. It was such an unhappy experience that when Archie headed back to the Vikings the following season in 1985, Olivia and the boys voted to stay in New Orleans.

"It's too cold up there," Peyton told his mother.

The oldest son, Cooper, was born two years before Peyton. The two of them were always close friends—but even closer rivals. No matter what they competed in, if Cooper won, Peyton cried. And in those early days, Cooper always won.

"He was kind of a baby," Olivia said of how Peyton handled his defeats by his older brother. "Peyton liked to tell on Cooper, like, 'Mommy, Cooper did so and so.'"

Archie tried to delay his sons' involvement in football, saying it was too rough a sport for such youngsters. But he certainly knew all three boys eventually would wind up playing the game.

Cooper started out at quarterback in elementary school. He played on a fifth-grade school team. Peyton, then in the third grade and too young to suit up, was the team manager. By the time Cooper reached high school age, he had switched to receiver. Cooper attended Isidore Newman School, a private school that all three Manning boys attended straight through twelfth grade. Cooper, whose best sport might have been basketball, quickly realized that the quarterback for Newman was going to be his younger brother.

Although Newman was a private academy, it played against public schools, so its sports programs were well known throughout New Orleans and Louisiana. Of course, having two sons of a former NFL quarterback and a legend throughout the South did not hurt Newman's program a bit. Archie made sure Peyton understood what kind of spotlight he would be in.

"People are going to compare you to me in high school," Archie Manning told his son, "and when you go to college they're going to compare you to whoever came before you, and to me."

In Peyton's sophomore season and Cooper's senior year at Newman, they were an unstoppable duo. In guiding the school to the state semifinals, Peyton completed 140 passes, 80 of them to Cooper.

"It was like being in the back yard and drawing up plays in the dirt," Peyton said. "We had our own signals. It's the most fun I've ever had playing football."

"That season," Cooper added, "brought us together as brothers."

Cooper followed Archie's path to the University of Mississippi. But after sitting out his freshman season to learn the Ole Miss offense, Cooper was found to have spinal stenosis. The neck injury meant he would never play football again.

"I went to college to play football and, all of a sudden, it's over and what do I do now?" Cooper said.

Cooper Manning would graduate from Mississippi with a degree in communications. He would be just fine without football.

But would Ole Miss football be fine without Cooper's brother, Peyton? Understanding how much pressure would be placed on him if he tried to play the same position at the same college where his father was such a hero, Peyton chose to attend Tennessee. It was an announcement widely

Peyton Manning's parents, Archie and Olivia Manning, are pictured in 1996.

cheered in Knoxville, Tennessee, and roundly booed in Oxford, Mississippi.

Although Archie and Olivia certainly supported any decision Peyton made, they were not about to steer him in one direction.

"I didn't want to go anywhere where I would be a star without doing anything," Peyton admitted. "That's what would have happened at Ole Miss."

While Peyton was headed for a record-setting career at Tennessee, the third Manning boy, Eli, was about to step in as Newman's quarterback. He was comfortable right from the beginning, just like Peyton. He had a smooth delivery, stood tall in the pocket, and could throw every kind of pass.

In his three years as Newman's starter, Eli threw for 7,389 yards and 89 touchdowns. When he could get a break from college—or later on, from the Colts—Peyton would join Archie, Olivia, and Cooper at Eli's games. Peyton even would study film with Eli.

Peyton also knew that Eli would have an even tougher decision about which college to attend. After all, Peyton had to deal with just his father's fame. Eli had a father and a brother who were among the greatest college quarterbacks in history. Archie was not sure what Eli would decide, especially with both Ole Miss and Tennessee showing strong interest in his youngest son.

"Yes, I'd love for him to go to Mississippi and play for them. I would have loved for Peyton to go to Ole Miss, but I wanted him to make the decision of what was best for him and Tennessee certainly worked out fine," Archie said. "Our entire family wants Eli to make his decision on the same basis."

Eli decided to make his commitment before Christmas of his senior year at Newman.

Archie Manning stands with his family at midfield during halftime of a Saints game on December 20, 1993. From left to right are Eli, Peyton, Olivia, Archie, and Cooper, who is seen accepting an award on his father's behalf.

"That was his plan from the start," Archie said. "He always said he didn't want it messing up his Christmas holidays."

Eli's choice? Ole Miss—although he would not wear the No. 18 his father wore, but rather No. 10. Archie believed being compared to Peyton at Tennessee simply would have been too much of a distraction for Eli.

"The Peyton years at Tennessee were recent and productive, and now he's a pro player," Archie said. "There are a whole bunch of, not only college kids, but young adults who don't remember me."

Eli did not struggle with the fame attached to the Manning name. His coach at Ole Miss, David Cutcliffe, was Peyton's offensive coordinator at Tennessee. When he moved on to the job at Mississippi, Cutcliffe immediately made Eli Manning his highest recruiting priority. Cutcliffe knew that Eli could handle the pressure as well as Peyton had throughout his college career.

"We talk about it," Cutcliffe said. "That's part of the expectations and part of trying to be as good a player as you can be. You can't run from those things."

"Eli stays focused. He does know his name is Manning and that he's at Ole Miss, but I don't think that hinders him."

While Cooper Manning lost his shot at professional football stardom and Peyton is experiencing the ups and downs of the NFL, Eli is the football future of the family. What would it be like to someday see Eli on one side of an NFL field and Peyton on the other? Peyton and Eli would like to find out.

"I can call him and talk to him about things that not many others can," Eli said. "He's another quarterback, a brother and a friend. It's made us closer."

Added Peyton, "That would be really special to play against Eli. We'll just have to see how things go.

"But I know one thing: It would be real tough on my mom and dad trying to root for one of us."

Chapter 3

Early College Years

Much was expected of Peyton Manning when he arrived at the University of Tennessee in Knoxville. Manning delivered on nearly every count.

He was going to be the greatest passer in school history—and he was.

He was going to lead the Volunteers to the top of the Southeastern Conference—and he did.

He was going to become a folk hero in the state—and he did.

And Manning would become an All-American, just like his father. He did that, too.

In all, Manning would set thirty-three Tennessee quarterback records. He would break the conference records for most victories (39 in 45 games), most completions, most yards passing, most total offense, best completion percentage, lowest interception percentage, and most 300-yard games. Consider that such great passers as Joe Namath, Bart Starr, Steve Spurrier, Fran Tarkenton—and, of course, Archie Manning—played in the SEC. Yet Peyton Manning outpassed them all.

Manning even outdid star college quarterbacks from other schools in other areas of the nation. He set the

NCAA record for lowest career interception percentage, and also established the single-season mark in that category when only 4 of his 380 passes were picked off in 1995, his sophomore season.

"For anyone who says throwing the ball isn't the safe way to play, I know they didn't have Peyton as their quarterback," Volunteers coach Phillip Fulmer said.

Manning's freshman season began early, as he enrolled in summer school in July 1994. The idea was to get a head start on his studies and his football career. Peyton knew that if he became comfortable with being in college right away, he would have a better chance of playing as a freshman.

Manning missed much of the social life a college freshman usually enjoys because he was so focused on football. He spent so much time studying film of games that his teammates called him "Caveman."

Eventually, Manning's studying paid off. Tennessee's starting quarterback the previous year, Heath Shuler, had entered the NFL after his junior season, so the job was wide open. Manning's competition included senior Jerry Colquitt (the favorite to start), junior Todd Helton, and another highly recruited freshman out of Texas, Brandon Stewart.

Manning was on the bench for the season opener at UCLA, a nationally televised game. Colquitt started and, in the first quarter, tore up his knee. Helton replaced him, but coach Fulmer told both Manning and Stewart that they would get in the game.

Manning was stunned. He wanted to play, of course, but he never expected to see action in the season opener, his very first game as a collegian. But after Helton struggled and UCLA went ahead 17–0, Fulmer put in Manning, whose one series did not go anywhere. Then Stewart came back in. Eventually, it was Helton who finished the game as the Vols lost, 25–23.

"We weren't trying to play musical quarterbacks by any stretch of the imagination. We were trying to get ready for the season and next season," Fulmer said. "I made the decision not just for this year, but also for next year that the more experience those two guys can get, the better."

Manning was disappointed that one series was all the time he got. Still, he had gotten a taste of being the quarterback of one of the best college squads in the nation. And he wanted more. Much more.

"I liked the way it felt to be on the field, even for just three plays. I really didn't think I would play so soon, anyway."

Peyton had become close with offensive coordinator David Cutcliffe, who would become his main advisor and a close friend through the years. That helped Manning tremendously, because he had so much confidence in Cutcliffe, who was an excellent teacher of quarterbacks. And Manning was the best prospect Cutcliffe had ever seen. As Cutcliffe recalled:

> Peyton benefited greatly just from the way he was raised. He benefited first as a person from the good things he was taught, and secondly as a player. Being Archie's son, he learned a lot about how to handle the situations around football, the hoopla, the challenges, the good and bad that go with being a quarterback, and keep on a level emotionally.

In the fourth game, Helton injured his knee at Mississippi State. His season was over. Fulmer turned to Manning, but this time for more than one series. On his third play against UCLA, Manning had been sacked. On his third play against Mississippi State, he hit Kendrick Jones for a 76-yard touchdown. Unfortunately, the Vols lost again, even though Manning completed 14 of 23 passes for 256 yards and 2 touchdowns.

"I felt good out there. I really did. I felt poised," said Manning, who was not particularly popular in the state after opting to go to Tennessee and not follow in his father's footsteps at Ole Miss. "Mississippi is somewhat my home turf. I tried to do a good job. But the loss, it hurts bad." Tennessee had turnovers on its last four drives, although Manning did not commit any. "The loss, it kills me. We had a real chance. We should have won the game, but it got away from us."

Archie Manning missed what was the beginning of a fabulous career because he attended Eli's game that day. It would be the only college game of Peyton's career that Archie did not attend.

The Volunteers came on later in the '94 season as Manning improved. After their 1–3 start, they won seven of their next eight games with Peyton as the No. 1 quarterback. Then they defeated Virginia Tech 45–23 in the Gator Bowl and finished ranked No. 22 nationally.

Peyton was honored as the SEC's top freshman. Many people considered him the best freshman in the nation.

"That was flattering," Peyton said, "but it didn't mean our team would get any more wins."

Manning knew one thing that would lead to more victories, maybe to an SEC title and then to a national championship: hard work. So even during summers, when most college students are at the beach or camping in the mountains or just plain goofing off, Manning was working out. New Orleans can get very hot and muggy during the summer, but that never stopped Peyton Manning.

"I remember one day when he was at Tennessee, he and I were the only two in the weight room," said Jim Mora, then the coach of the NFL's New Orleans Saints. Mora later would become coach of the Colts and would be Peyton's first head coach in the pros. "I'm watching him lift and he's lifting like some big old lineman. Not like a quarterback. He was really getting into it. He loves to lift."

It was not just weight work that interested Manning. Just as in high school, when he practiced with NFL players to get better, Manning was eager to keep sharp while in college. So he took every opportunity to get out on a field and throw, to find other players who would run pass patterns for him.

He spent time studying film and the Volunteers' playbook. In his mind, he would devise plays he thought the coaching staff might use in games.

"I think it's fun to see what more you can learn in the film room, or how much better you can get in the weight room or throwing the football," he said. "I had that work ethic instilled in me at a young age, and I keep trying to take that to the next level."

In 1995, the starting job was Manning's, with no threat from any other quarterback, because Stewart had trans-ferred to Texas A&M. Coach Fulmer would open up the offense to allow Manning more freedom to pass. Manning knew he had to produce and lead the Vols to a better record and a more prestigious bowl game.

By now, everyone in Knoxville knew what everyone in New Orleans had learned long ago. The rest of the nation was about to find out, as well, that Peyton Manning did not back down from such challenges.

"I don't know if it has anything to do with being fair or not," Cutcliffe said. "Obviously expectations are big. It's something we've talked about. I think he's got to focus on being the best he can be, and he'll do that. That's all you can ask."

As a sophomore, Peyton was superb in class, getting a 3.5 average out of a possible 4.0. And he was sensational on the field, passing for 22 touchdowns and nearly 3,000 yards. He completed 64 percent and averaged just one interception every 95 throws. Tennessee finished 11–1 and No. 3 in the final poll.

But there were some negatives for the school's football program that season. Fulmer disciplined twenty-nine players for their part in a telephone scandal. (All told, thirty-one athletes were disciplined. The university said about 17,000 calls were made over about a year using the stolen long-distance access code of an athletic department employee. Manning was not involved.) Once again, the Vols lost to archrival Florida, this time after building a 30–14 lead. By the time the Gators were through with the Vols, they had scored 48 straight points to win 62–37.

That meant no SEC championship for Tennessee, which wound up second to Florida. But there were wins over Georgia and Alabama, two schools Tennessee rarely beat in the same season. In fact, the Vols routed Alabama 41–14 as part of an eight-game winning streak.

And there was a trip to Orlando for the Citrus Bowl, played on New Year's Day. The Volunteers beat powerful Ohio State 20–14. But the fact that Florida played for the national championship, losing to Nebraska, ate away at the Vols.

"Eleven-and-one is something you're pleased with, but that one just sticks right in your craw," Fulmer said.

Everyone at Tennessee believed the next season, Peyton's junior year, would be perfect. Of course, placing such high expectations—demanding nothing less than a spotless record and a national title—was absurd. With the difficult schedule the Volunteers play every year, how could anyone predict perfection?

Yet people did.

Tennessee was ranked No. 2 in the preseason polls, meaning the Vols were expected to battle for the national title in the Sugar Bowl. That game is played in Manning's hometown of New Orleans. In addition, Manning was

Peyton Manning goes back to pass during a Tennessee Volunteers game.

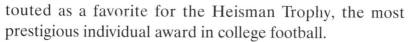

touted as a favorite for the Heisman Trophy, the most prestigious individual award in college football.

So there were traps set everywhere for Manning and the Volunteers. Peyton recognized them, especially after talking to tight ends coach Rodney Garner and receivers coach Pat Washington. Both of them had played at Auburn, which was considered a lock for the national championship in 1985, when the great Bo Jackson was on the team. Auburn did not win it.

"Coach Garner told me you've got to watch it," Manning admitted. "He said they had unbelievable talent on that team, but had 22 individuals. Everybody has to stay together, work towards one main goal. It's something that can easily happen. Guys start believing they're on the best team and start doing something they don't normally do, and you start losing ballgames."

Washington warned the players not to look at the rankings.

"That puts you in the area where you have a chance to compete for the national championship, but you can't live off of last year," he said. "Also, it means every team you play will be gunning for you. They'll play better than what you see on the film."

It did not take long for Manning and the Vols to discover that. After victories against Nevada-Las Vegas and UCLA in which Manning played well, the Vols played Florida. Florida had won three straight against Tennessee.

The winner would have the inside track to the SEC championship—and maybe the national title. Adding interest to the matchup was the Heisman Trophy race, in which Manning and Florida's Danny Wuerffel were considered the top quarterbacks.

"I'm not about Heisman. I'm about wins and losses," Manning insisted. "This Florida game, I would love to go

0-for-25 and have a big win. That would be perfectly fine with me."

Unfortunately for Manning, he nearly did play that badly. And his team got a big loss. Manning threw 4 interceptions and fumbled once. Florida raced out to a 35–0 lead before winning 35-29.

"I'm just sorry it was against Florida," Manning said. "I feel bad for so many people, for the fans this game meant so much to. It meant a lot to me also. I'm sorry I played the way I did. I'm very disappointed."

He would also be disappointed when the Volunteers, as 26-point favorites, were shocked by cross-state rival Memphis, which beat Tennessee for the first time ever.

"Any competitor hates to lose a game you should have won. But Memphis played great football and just flat whipped us," said Manning, who was 23-of-40 for 296 yards and a touchdown, but also threw 2 interceptions.

Even worse, Manning sprained his right knee in a victory over Arkansas the next week. Although he did not miss any games, even leading the Vols to a 48-28 win over Northwestern in the Citrus Bowl to finish 10–2, Manning felt he was not at his best. Still, his play was good enough to impress everybody else.

"He had an exceptional season and exhibited a great amount of toughness by playing the last three games with a ligament tear in his knee," Fulmer said. "He didn't have to play, but he did, and we won all three of them."

Although he made third-team All-American and finished eighth in the Heisman Trophy voting, the season left him with an empty feeling. And it left him facing some very big questions.

Chapter 4

Senior Year

Chad Plummer was a college quarterback at the University of Cincinnati who eventually would be a reserve wide receiver with the Colts. When he was in school, his coaches gave him specific instructions.

"My coach had me watch tape of Peyton in college," he said. "I used to watch tapes and read articles on him all the time. I used to try to imitate him in college, but I couldn't get it done.

"Not many people can do what Peyton can do."

Not many people can graduate in three years with a 3.61 grade point average. Or make the Academic All-America team three times. Peyton had done that. So the natural question was: Why stay at Tennessee for his senior year of eligibility when he could enter the NFL draft and be the first player chosen?

That left Manning with a difficult choice.

"The way I look at it, it's kind of an honor to be able to graduate in three years," he said. "I feel I've earned the right to take my time, research it and make the best decision possible."

There were dozens of factors that would enter into his decision. If he turned pro, he almost certainly would wind up with the New York Jets, coached by Bill Parcells. That was attractive to Peyton and his father, who knew Parcells well and believed he would be an excellent coach for Peyton.

If he stayed at Tennessee, he could enjoy college life without needing to carry around books or attend classes, because he already had graduated. He could have fun!

Turning pro would make him a very rich young man, and he would enter the NFL as a healthy quarterback. Returning to Knoxville would mean another college season in which he might be injured, damaging his potential as a pro.

Peyton took several months examining all sides before calling a news conference for March 5, 1997. He had not hinted about his decision and, before a hushed crowd in Knoxville, Manning said: "I made up my mind and I don't expect to ever look back. I am going to stay at the University of Tennessee."

Cheers went up around the room.

"As difficult as it has been I knew I couldn't make a bad decision. But I knew whatever decision I made had to be my own decision and nobody else's."

Even Parcells, whose team lost out most by Manning's decision, applauded it.

"I think the common feeling in this country today is that everybody sells out for the money and the opportunity. I think that in Peyton's case, I admire his decision and think that it took courage to make it, and I wish him well. I think things will go well for him," Parcells said. "I'm very respectful of him. I think it's refreshing, really."

The Tennessee Legislature thought so, too, passing a resolution that said: "In this time of unbridled greed and diminished loyalty, it is indeed refreshing to see a young man honor his commitments to his school and his teammates. He represents everything that is admirable about our young people today."

And why, exactly, did Manning decide to stay?

"Twenty-five, $30 million. I'm human. Believe me, I looked at the money," he said. "I'm hoping the money's there next year, too, the good Lord willing I stay healthy. But staying was strongest in my heart. I knew that's what I wanted to do.

"Sure I hope to win a championship, but I promise you that's not the reason I came back. This is just something I wanted to do. I wanted to come back and be a college student one more year."

With that settled, Manning got ready for his senior season, in which he would be a Heisman Trophy favorite and the Vols would be one of the top choices to win the national championship.

The schedule began against Texas Tech and Manning looked like, well, a pro. He threw for 310 yards and 5 touchdowns in a 52–17 romp. (And he did not even play in the fourth quarter!)

Next up was a trip to the Rose Bowl to play UCLA, the site of Manning's college debut. Manning wanted to put on a big show before a national television audience. He did that early on, guiding the Vols to a 24–3 lead. He struggled in the fourth quarter, but Tennessee held on to win 30–24.

At 2–0, the Vols headed to Gainesville for the annual matchup with Florida. It would be Manning's last chance to beat the Gators, against whom he had had some of his worst performances.

"People think it's a big psychological thing, but it really isn't," Manning said. "I think mentally the past few years we've been very sound. Our focus has been good. It's just physically we haven't gone out there on Saturday and gotten the job done."

Nor would they do the job this time. Although Manning completed 29 of 51 passes for 353 yards and 3 touchdowns, he also had 2 passes intercepted. Florida's Tony George returned one 89 yards for a touchdown.

Peyton Manning shows his frustration after a Tennessee loss.

In three starts against the Gators, Manning threw for 1,171 yards, 8 touchdowns, and 6 interceptions.

"I am disappointed, but I didn't come back just for this game. There is a lot of football to be played," he said. "I'm disappointed for our fans, our coaches and for our seniors who have never beaten Florida. I needed to play extremely well to win this ballgame, and I didn't do that."

Manning would not let the loss to Florida destroy his year. Instead, he set about having the best season of his college career. The Vols won their next eight regular-season games as Manning posted big numbers. They scored at least 31 points five times, getting 59 against Kentucky as Manning went 25-for-35 for 523 yards and 5 touchdowns. The touchdowns all came in the first three periods, covering distances of 17, 31, 50, 59, and 66 yards. The total yards passing set a school record, as did his 12 straight completions early in the game.

The winning streak lifted Tennessee into the SEC Championship game against Auburn. It also made Manning a co-favorite with Michigan cornerback Charles Woodson for the Heisman Trophy. But Peyton Manning wanted the SEC title and a shot at the national championship a lot more than the Heisman. As Manning himself stated:

> People think I really want to win this award [the Heisman]. People think I need this award. That really isn't the truth. I was never taught to play for individual awards. I don't want to take anything away from the award. I know it would be an honor to receive it. I respect the people who have won it before. For me personally, it's not that important.

First came the matchup with Auburn, which went a surprising 8–3 and won the SEC West. The Vols were heavily favored, but they trailed all game.

In the fourth quarter, Manning's final chance for a conference title was on the line. Displaying everything that made him a great quarterback, Peyton found Marcus Nash for a 73-yard touchdown down the right sideline at the Georgia Dome. That provided the winning points, and the Vols won the Southeastern Conference.

"It's a great feeling," Manning said. "This says something about the character of our team."

The Vols were headed for a showdown with Nebraska at the Orange Bowl. A victory could lift them to their first national championship since 1951.

Before that game, though, Manning headed to New York for the Heisman Trophy announcement. Fulmer had no doubt who should win.

"The character, integrity, and leadership are a representation of what college football should be about," Fulmer said. "Plus, with the numbers he's put up, there's no question in my mind that Peyton Manning is the best player in the country."

Others did have questions—enough others with enough questions that Woodson edged Manning for the award.

Manning did not worry. The Heisman was no big deal—not after putting together such a strong senior season and having a street in Knoxville renamed "Peyton Manning Pass."

"All I've ever tried to do here was to be a good, loyal team member," he said. "I've missed one practice in my career. I've always taken pride in that. I've come to work every single day, tried to get better and tried to help my team win games."

The Orange Bowl would be the last game of his college career. With a victory, it would be the most satisfying. But the Vols were matched up against a Nebraska powerhouse that was unbeaten and ranked number one in the polls.

Peyton Manning scrambles out of the pocket during a Volunteers game in September 1997.

The Cornhuskers showed why by routing the Vols 42–17. They, not Manning's team, would be national champions.

It was a bitter way to end a wonderful four years at Knoxville. Manning had a poor game, throwing for just 134 yards and one touchdown, with one interception. There were tears in his eyes when he looked back.

"So many memories," he said. "Tennessee has been good to me. I can't pay them back enough, the great things they've done for me. I'll always be a Tennessee Volunteer the rest of my life."

Peyton's father, Archie, who knew all about falling short of goals established by others, did not believe his son came up short on any count.

"I think he had an impact on others, and I'm glad it worked out for him," Archie Manning said. "He stayed healthy, won a conference championship, and we're glad he stayed. We're proud of him."

There would be many more opportunities for the Mannings to be proud of their son. Just five weeks after the Orange Bowl disappointment, Peyton won the prestigious Sullivan Award, given to the nation's outstanding amateur athlete by the Amateur Athletic Union. He was just the fourth football player to capture the honor since it was first awarded in 1930.

"Peyton's been very fortunate to win some real nice awards this year," Archie said. "This certainly is right up there with them. It's a little different than a football award. It's really special."

It was a fitting way for Peyton Manning to head to the NFL.

Chapter 5

Turning Pro

Peyton Manning would quickly learn that being selected first overall in the draft was the easiest part of being an NFL rookie.

After the Colts chose him, they immediately announced that Manning would be their starting quarterback. Rarely does that happen, even for the top pick, because the move from college football to the pros is such a huge step.

"The sooner you take your bumps and bruises, the better off that team will be in the long run," Manning said. "I do have some knowledge about the game, but from college to the NFL, it is the biggest adjustment possible. The speed of the game is so much faster. The defenses are so much more aggressive. Hopefully, my experiences will help me out."

Because Manning had gotten his degree from Tennessee in 1997, he asked the NFL to allow him to report early to the Colts so he could begin working with his new teammates. The league denied his request, so Manning moved out of his apartment in Knoxville and went back to his parents' home in New Orleans. He had to wait until June 1 before joining the team, which made no sense to his dad.

"He could also go in with the quarterback coach and the offensive coordinator and spend an hour, two hours every day continuing to learn their offense," Archie Manning said. "It would be very beneficial."

Not surprisingly, Peyton felt the same way. Known for his strong work ethic—how else could he have finished college so quickly while also playing football under such a spotlight?—Manning has always hated being idle:

> I've always believed you have to get prepared to play. It would be a bad feeling after a game if you say, "You know, I should have spent a little more time in my playbook and I should have studied a little more film." Or if you see that you should have worked out a little bit harder in the offseason. That would be a bad feeling. I don't ever want to have that.

Peyton Manning would have plenty of rough times as a rookie. But first, he was able to enjoy the Manning family atmosphere once again, hanging out with his brothers, childhood friends, and parents in New Orleans.

"I think that's when he really began to realize that his life was undergoing some major changes," Archie Manning said. "He made many good friends and has many great memories from his days in Knoxville. It's been fun these past few weeks having Peyton around the family. My wife and sons have added some enjoyable memories during the month. Family and football are the two most important parts of his life. He's been able to mix the two in May. However, he's ready for what lies ahead."

What was ahead was an enormous learning experience, beginning when Manning finally joined the Colts for a minicamp. It was there that he first began practicing with the receivers and running backs and blockers who would be his helpers in Indianapolis. It was there that he first felt like a professional athlete.

Manning's six-year contract gave him an $11.6 million signing bonus in a deal that was worth nearly $48 million. He was going to be rich, financially set for life.

But what really affected him was that now football was his job. A great job, for sure, but still work. And there was only one way to handle it.

"I don't think I'm being paid to set records, and stats. I came into this league to win football games," Manning said. "My number one goal in this league is to be a winner."

Winning was not likely to come too soon. The Colts earned the right to pick first in the draft by going 3–13. Their offense was weak, their defense filled with holes.

New coach Jim Mora had one star, running back Marshall Faulk; a bunch of unproven youngsters; and a rookie quarterback whom everyone would be watching closely. His team was playing in the difficult AFC East, and the first three regular-season games were against divisional opponents. But Mora knew that as long as Manning did not get frustrated or lose faith, better times were ahead.

Those better times seemed very near when Manning's first pass in his first exhibition game went for a 48-yard touchdown to Marvin Harrison. Manning and Harrison would become one of the most dangerous pass-catch combinations in the NFL, and this was a great way to start.

But those better times would seem far away when the Colts struggled in the preseason, losing three of four. And, as Peyton said, "the season was downhill from there."

Manning faced the difficult task of playing the Miami Dolphins and Dan Marino in his very first regular-season NFL game. Marino was not only pro football's career passing leader and a definite Hall-of-Famer, but one of Manning's favorite quarterbacks. Peyton knew there'd be comparisons between the great veteran and the raw rookie.

It was no contest—nor should it have been. Manning lacked the experience and comfort zone that Marino had

Peyton Manning launches a deep pass in a game against the Buffalo Bills on November 22, 1998, his rookie season.

built through the years. The Dolphins won easily and Manning threw 3 interceptions. But he also threw the first TD pass of his NFL career, to Harrison. It would be the first of many hookups for the duo.

It was an uneasy debut for Peyton Manning. He was very upset when he saw tapes of the game that showed how his father reacted in the stands. Archie discovered he needed to watch the games in privacy, away from the cameras, and not show so much emotion when things went wrong.

Things got even worse the next three weeks, including blowout road losses against the Patriots and Jets. Football was not any fun for Manning, who hardly ever was the losing quarterback in the past. And coming up were the Chargers in a game being hyped as Manning vs. Leaf, Draft Pick No. 1 vs. Draft Pick No. 2.

The Colts were 0–4, the Chargers 2–2, but Leaf already had made enemies in San Diego with his selfishness and lack of dedication to his job. Manning, despite the losses, was praised for his hard work and pleasant attitude.

"Peyton gets mad. He gets frustrated. Inside it hurts him to lose and not play well," Mora said. "But he handles it well. When he does throw the interception he'll run over and try and tackle the guy, not throw his helmet down. I think he'll stay positive. He has not gotten down. He has not regressed, or had his confidence shaken."

Manning had not lost hope despite the slow start. He liked the idea that people were paying attention to the Colts, even if they were focusing too much on his matchup with Leaf and not enough on everyone else.

And when the Colts beat the Chargers 17–12, there was much relief in Indianapolis—although neither Manning nor Leaf played particularly well.

"This week we finally put one away and won one," Manning said. "It's good to get a win and know we are capable of doing it."

As for the rivalry with Leaf, Manning added, "It's always going to be there, the comparison. You kind of get to accept it."

Manning refused to accept the losing, but as his father had taught him, patience in professional sports is the strongest of virtues. So even though the Colts could not get much going in Peyton's first NFL season, the young quarterback tried not to let his spirits get down.

"Sure, it leaves a bitter taste in your mouth," he said of the losses. "They get tougher and tougher as you play them closer and closer. You feel like you deserve to win." But looking at the positive side, he added, "I think that will help in a lot of ways. The guys will come back more determined."

Peyton Manning certainly would. With the mounting losses, the Colts would finish the season 3–13, Manning decided he would simply rededicate himself every week. That was what he was taught by his parents: work hard, remain focused, and never give up.

Perhaps Coach Mora was the first member of the Colts to see that Manning would not let up. As far back as the first minicamp, he noticed something special about his rookie quarterback:

> When he first got to minicamp, we were just going over some basic things that we talk about every year, stuff like meeting times and making living arrangements. Then I look up and I see Peyton's taking notes on this stuff and it was just a little odd. But once you're around him for a period of time and you see how disciplined he is and how much he cares, you realize that everything he does is with a purpose and that purpose is to be the best possible football player he can be.

Manning tries to beat the Baltimore Ravens secondary with a long throw during a game on November 29, 1998.

Although Peyton's first NFL season certainly was not memorable for the team's record, there were many lessons learned that would help him in the future. And his personal numbers were great: a rookie record of 3,739 yards passing and 26 touchdowns. Only All-Pros Brett Favre and Steve Young passed for more yardage that season. He also was on the field for every play, reading defenses, figuring out the strengths and weaknesses in them, and finding out just what his teammates were capable of.

Manning made several All-Rookie squads, while Leaf was a bust in San Diego. Not just among the Colts, but throughout the NFL Manning had impressed observers.

"The good Lord and his father made him a great quarterback," said Bruce Arians, who was his quarterback coach in 1998. "He's got the genes and the background to handle the NFL. That goes a lot farther than arm strength. You've got to have true grit and toughness to play in this league. You put that in a good body with a great brain, and you've got a heck of a player."

Added Colts president Bill Polian, the man who chose Manning over Leaf in the draft: "I wouldn't trade Peyton for any guy in this league. I've never seen anyone like Peyton except Dan Marino. To come into this league like he has is unheard of."

"This is my job and I take this very seriously," Manning said. "They pay me a lot of money, so I take that very seriously, too . . . I'm in this for the long haul, and I hope my hard work will pay off for me."

Chapter 6

The Turnaround

One thing the Colts knew they must do in Peyton Manning's second NFL season was get more help for him. And when they traded away their best player, do-everything running back Marshall Faulk, it made people wonder what was going on.

But the Colts were afraid they would soon lose Faulk as a free agent. And they fully planned to draft a running back to replace Faulk and fit in with Manning and star receiver Marvin Harrison to form a Terrific Trio on offense.

A debate waged over who was a better pro prospect, Heisman Trophy winner Ricky Williams of Texas or Miami running back Edgerrin James. Colts president Bill Polian looked at dozens of factors: Who was a better receiver? Who blocked better? Who was more of a team player? Who had performed better in big games?

Polian also spoke to Dr. Robert Troutwine, an industrial psychologist in Liberty, Missouri, who gives mental tests to likely NFL draftees. Dr. Troutwine told Polian that James was a better match for his team than Williams, because James could handle having a bigger star—Manning—on the team.

The Colts took James with the fourth overall pick in the draft, one spot ahead of Williams. Manning's reaction?

"I see him very similar to Marshall in a lot of ways. He catches the ball well out of the backfield, but he can pound it in there on third-and-1. Bill and the entire scouting staff thought this was the right decision. Obviously, they know a lot about him."

Having gone through the rigors of being a high draft choice, Manning knew how difficult the adjustment to the NFL could be for James, who left college after his junior season.

"Edgerrin is going to have a lot of pressure on him, both nationally and locally," Peyton said. "I think he's a good kid . . . he's been through a lot, from where he grew up, a lot of tough times in his life. I think mentally he'll be able to handle it."

Things started well for Manning and the Colts in 1999. They routed Buffalo, usually the favorite in the AFC East. And they played well in losing a close game to New England in which Patriots star quarterback Drew Bledsoe, the top overall draft pick in 1993, was impressed by Manning.

"He was definitely more successful in his rookie season than I was. I think he had maybe the best rookie season of any quarterback ever," Bledsoe said. "Peyton looks very good. He progressed very quickly. They have to continue to develop the team around him. I've been fortunate enough with the Patriots to have some very good teams around me, and if they can continue to develop the players around Peyton, I think he's got all the ability to take them to where they want to be."

Develop they did. James quickly moved to the top of the NFL rushing charts. Harrison was among the leading receivers. Manning was among the most dangerous passers.

Manning releases the ball just in time to avoid a sack during a game against the San Diego Chargers on September 26, 1999.

Even with a so-so defense, the Colts began winning. Manning set a franchise record of 404 yards passing as the Colts snapped a 10-game road losing streak by beating San Diego. He was selected the AFC's Offensive Player of the Week for that performance.

"I'm certainly excited with the way things are going," said Manning. "We certainly wanted to see improvement from last year and eliminate some of the mistakes that we made last year. We are making a lot more plays than we did last year. That certainly is encouraging."

Manning calls the play at the line of scrimmage during a game from September 1999.

Colts fans would be more encouraged as the season went on. By mid-November, the team had won five straight for the first time since 1992. When they won their sixth in a row, the Colts were 8–2 and in first place. James led the AFC in rushing and Harrison was at the top in receiving. Manning was making all the right decisions on the field. As Manning said:

> Confidence is certainly the biggest thing. I'm certainly a more confident quarterback. I'm using the experience of last year to my advantage, and the team is more confident we can win every single ballgame. Last year we hoped we could win games. This year we really do believe we can win, and that helps you play better.

James was headed for something Peyton Manning did not win the previous season: Offensive Rookie of the Year.

"He is such a threat in all phases of the game, running inside, running outside, short yardage, on the goal line, and now he's a big threat in the passing game," Manning said of James. "I really feel the defense has to account for him on every single play."

The Colts were on such a roll that they began thinking not just about making the playoffs, but about winning their first division title since 1987. After beating the Jets, Dolphins, and Patriots to take full control of the AFC East, the Colts took aim at the best record in the league.

"Because of where we are and what we can accomplish with one more win in these next three games, our goals are certainly a lot further than just making the playoffs," coach Jim Mora said.

Manning was excited at the prospect of leading a team that was 3–13 for two straight years into the Super Bowl chase. He was having a terrific season, one that would land him in the Pro Bowl along with the great quarterbacks of the game. His father, Archie, never came close to a championship while playing for the New Orleans Saints, Minnesota Vikings, and Houston Oilers.

"A lot of people had the idea that we'd be going as a wild-card," Manning said. "And now, we have the chance of winning the division, so we're pretty excited about that. . . . This team is still very hungry."

So hungry that they beat Washington 24–21 to wrap up the division. And so hungry that, with a win against Cleveland, they achieved the best turnaround in NFL history: from 3–13 to 13–3.

Manning set franchise records of 331 completions and 4,135 yards. He had a streak of 27 straight games with a TD pass. The Colts had the top-ranked offense in all of football, thanks in large part to Peyton Manning.

But it was not enough to win the team's first NFL crown since the 1971 season. Maybe the Colts were too young. Certainly, the defense was not equal to the high-powered offense.

Indianapolis lost its playoff game at home to Tennessee, 19–16. Manning struggled against the Titans' strong defense, which would help Tennessee win the AFC title. He completed only 19 of 42 passes for 227 yards and did not throw for a touchdown. He did run for a TD near the end of the game, but it was not enough.

"You've got to have big plays against playoff teams," Manning said before making a promise. "It's something we'll learn, and I believe we'll be back next year."

Chapter 7

Up and Down

By his third NFL season, Peyton Manning was a star. He had become one of pro sports' most popular players—not just among the football crowd, but in all sports. Manning, however, was not much interested in stardom. His sights were set on something else: championships.

First, he would have to improve on an already incredible season in which he led the Colts to the biggest turnaround in league history. After going from 3–13 to 13–3, the next logical step for Indianapolis was a Super Bowl.

Colts quarterbacks coach Bruce Arians knew that Manning would do everything he could to make it happen.

"He's like Tiger Woods," Arians said. "He's the last guy to leave the range. Peyton will stay out there and work with the guys until their legs fall off. That's the way he is."

Indeed, Manning was ready for more success in 2000. He was ready to go all the way.

"I'm proud that we've gotten things turned around," he said. "As a quarterback, what you're judged by isn't necessarily all the touchdowns and the yards, but winning games."

Surprisingly, the wins did not start coming the way Peyton and everyone else in Indianapolis expected. The Colts were just 3–2 after five weeks, meaning they would have to win 10 of their last 11 games to equal their 1999 record.

While Manning had some huge games early in the season—he threw for 440 yards and 4 touchdowns in a 43–14 rout of Jacksonville, and 367 yards and 3 scores in a 38–31 loss to Oakland—he also was throwing too many interceptions.

Even though Edgerrin James and Marvin Harrison also were nearly unstoppable, the defense struggled. It was obvious that the Colts would have to win a bunch of shootouts to get to the top. Fortunately, they had a quarterback who was up to the challenge.

In the next three weeks, the Colts scored 97 points in three games—and won every time. At the halfway point of the season, the Colts were 6–2. Led by Manning, they looked ready to do some damage in the standings.

"He wins," Jacksonville coach Tom Coughlin said. "Anybody who comes into this league and starts every game from his rookie year on and has the great turnaround that Indianapolis experienced, he's a winner."

In their next game against the Chicago Bears, the Colts fell behind early, 27–0. The team rallied, but came up short 27–24. The team bounced back quickly, beating the Jets at home, but losses in their next three games dropped them to 7–6. They were barely alive in the playoff race.

"It's disappointing," Manning said. "I think there's a big difference between being disappointed and being discouraged. We're disappointed with the losses, but when you get discouraged, that's when it carries over to the next week. Now we really do have to hope for some things to happen that are out of our control. And that's a position you don't want to be in."

The first thing the Colts needed to do was believe in themselves. Coach Jim Mora made sure that was a priority.

Manning runs with the ball during a game at Buffalo against the Bills in October 2000.

"If you have the right kind of people, you believe they'll fight through the season right till the end," he said.

They also needed an offensive spark, and James gave it to them in Game 14, running for 111 yards and 3 touchdowns in a 44–20 romp past the Bills. When the Jets and Dolphins lost, Indy had hope that they could make the playoffs.

The Colts, still in a must-win situation, also had a trip to Miami in Week 15. They were 8–23 at Miami in their history. But they also were desperate, and the defense came through this time with four sacks. While James ran for 112 yards, Manning passed for one TD and ran for another as the Colts won, 20–13.

The Jets cooperated by losing again. Suddenly, the playoff dream was alive again.

"We don't necessarily like being in this position," Manning said of needing a victory, plus a loss by either New York or Miami, to make the playoffs. "Instead of complaining about it and whining about it, we're trying to do something about it."

Manning already had become the fifth quarterback ever to pass for 4,000 yards in consecutive seasons. But personal glory meant little in such a nervous time.

The Colts finished their season with a dominating 31–10 victory over Minnesota. James had 128 yards to win his second straight rushing title. Manning threw for 4 TDs, three to Harrison, giving Peyton 33 TD passes, a team mark. The defense shut down the Vikings, and when the Jets lost to Baltimore, the Colts were a wild-card playoff team.

Manning had been selected AFC Offensive Player of the Week for the fourth time. He would not have minded repeating that feat in each of the next few games, if it meant getting the Colts to the Super Bowl.

"We have a lot of momentum, we have a lot of confidence. We won three games in must-win situations,

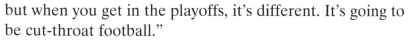

but when you get in the playoffs, it's different. It's going to be cut-throat football."

He looked like he might be ready to lead Indianapolis all the way to the championship during the first half of the playoff game at Miami. Manning sparked the Colts to a 14–0 lead, and they led 17–10 late in the game. But the defense tired and the Dolphins forced overtime by scoring a touchdown with just 34 seconds on the clock.

When reliable kicker Mike Vanderjagt missed a 49-yard field goal in overtime, it opened the door for the Dolphins. They burst through it as Lamar Smith scored on a 17-yard run to eliminate the Colts 23–17.

Manning and his teammates were crushed.

"Everybody is just frustrated. Looking back at it now, there were just a lot of missed opportunities. We got field goals and didn't get touchdowns."

Although it was a depressing way to end the season, hope remained strong in Indianapolis. As Coach Mora said, how could you feel too badly when you had the best young quarterback in football on your side?

"He'll get better. Heck, yeah, he'll get better. He just has to play, just get the experience and see all the situations that are out there through his career.

"I'm sure the confidence level will grow, feeling comfortable, those kinds of things. It's just a matter of maturing and getting experience and getting better."

Chapter 8

Growing Pains

In early 2001, Peyton Manning married Ashley Thompson, whom he began dating as a freshman at the University of Tennessee. About 600 people attended the wedding.

On the field, Colts coach Jim Mora recognized the need to improve the Indianapolis defense after it held back the team in 2000. So Mora and team president Bill Polian released five defensive starters. They signed some veteran free agents, plugged a couple of youngsters into the starting lineup, and drafted safety Idrees Bashir. When they were done, the Colts had six new starters on defense with a combined 11 NFL starts heading into the 2001 season.

Manning was hopeful the changes, plus some improvement from the offense, would make the Colts championship material.

"I'm in my fourth season and some of the other guys are veterans, but we're still a young team with a chance to grow," Manning said. "With the talent we have, if we can make as much progress as I think we can, we should be right in there."

Led by Peyton Manning, Indianapolis started strong. In their first two games, the Colts overpowered two division rivals, the Jets (45–24) and the Bills (42–26). The offense

Peyton Manning looks to hand off to the running back during a game in October 2000.

appeared unstoppable, and the defense was making enough good plays to have everyone thinking positive thoughts.

But the Colts lost their next three games, including twice to New England as the defense fell apart. Peyton struggled against the shifting defenses of the Patriots, whose coach, Bill Belichick, was well-known for his ability to confuse opposing quarterbacks. In a 44–13 loss at New England, Manning was intercepted three times—two of them were returned for touchdowns. It was as bad a loss as Peyton had ever experienced.

"You get depressed, try to make a play," Manning said. "That's what happened on Smith's interception. You either make the play or get burned. We got burned."

"We can't just throw in the towel right now," said star running back Edgerrin James. "We're 2–3 and we know that everybody is going to be against us, but we really can't worry about that. It is a long season."

With Manning leading the team, the Colts rebounded with victories against Kansas City and Buffalo in their next two games. However, James hurt his knee in one of the games and would not return. Linebacker Mike Peterson, the team's best defender, also was lost to a knee injury.

At 4–3 the Colts still had a chance to move back into the AFC East race as they hosted the Dolphins. Still smarting from their playoff defeat at Miami, the Colts were eager to get some revenge and prove themselves to be title contenders.

Manning and the Colts played tough, but wound up losing a close game, 27–24. Even worse, Manning suffered a broken jaw when hit helmet-to-helmet by the Dolphins' Lorenzo Bromell. While Bromell was fined by the league for the illegal hit that left Manning bloody and dazed, Peyton was stuck eating soup and drinking milkshakes for awhile.

Manning looks to pass against the Oakland Raiders in a game from September of 2000.

With injuries to key players mounting, the Colts struggled. The team lost its next two games against New Orleans and the high-powered San Francisco 49ers. Suddenly, they were 4–6 and falling quickly out of the playoff race.

For the final six weeks of the schedule, the Colts were playing out the string. They lost to Baltimore, Miami again, the Jets, and St. Louis, then beat Denver to finish 6–10. It was, without question, the most difficult season of Manning's young career.

Mora and his coaching staff were fired, meaning the Colts pretty much would be starting over in 2002. Mora knew just why the team failed in 2001: not enough talent.

"Peyton Manning is a great player . . . this year he became one of three quarterbacks to throw for 4,000 yards in three consecutive seasons. Do you know who the other two are? Dan Marino and Dan Fouts," Mora said. "Now can you tell me how many Super Bowls they won? None. It takes more than a great quarterback throwing for 4,000 yards every year to win a Super Bowl."

Peyton Manning is a very resilient and optimistic person and player. He is certain that the future holds much success for him and his team.

"We just need to pick ourselves up and be professionals," Manning said. "We need to look ahead, not behind."

As long as Peyton Manning is taking the snaps, you can be sure it will not be long before the Colts are back on top of the football world.

Career Statistics

College

Year	Team	Att	Comp	Pct	Yds	Td	Int
1994	Tennessee	144	89	61.8	1,141	11	6
1995	Tennessee	380	244	64.2	2,954	22	4
1996	Tennessee	380	243	63.9	3,287	20	12
1997	Tennessee	477	287	60.4	3,819	37	11
Totals		1,381	863	62.5	11,201	90	33

NFL

Year	Team	Games	Att	Comp	Pct	Yds	Td	Int
1998	Indianapolis	16	575	326	56.7	3,739	26	28
1999	Indianapolis	16	533	331	62.1	4,135	26	15
2000	Indianapolis	16	571	357	62.5	4,413	33	15
2001	Indianapolis	16	547	343	62.7	4,131	26	23
Totals		64	2,226	1,357	61.0	16,418	111	81

Att = Attempts   **Yds** = Yards
Comp = Completions **Td** = Touchdowns
Pct = Completion Percentage **Int** = Interceptions

Where to Write Peyton Manning

Mr. Peyton Manning
c/o The Indianapolis Colts
RCA Dome
100 S. Capitol Ave.
Indianapolis, IN 46225

On the Internet at:

http://www.peytonmanning.com
http://www.colts.com
http://www.nfl.com

Index